camilla LØW
STRAIGHT LETTERS

Camilla Løw
Straight Letters

Dundee Contemporary Arts
2 February–13 April 2008

Pier Arts Centre, Orkney
20 June–6 September 2008

First published in 2008 by
DCA, Dundee Contemporary Arts, 152 Nethergate,
Dundee, Scotland DD1 4DY

tel 01382 909 900 / fax 01382 909 221
mail@dca.org.uk / www.dca.org.uk

British Library Cataloguing-in-Publication Data
A British Library CIP record is available

ISBN13: 978-0-9558769-0-5

Exhibition curated and organised by
Judith Winter and Graham Domke

Text: Michael Archer and Dr Sarah Lowndes

Photography: Ruth Clark

Design: Robert Johnston

The DCA Director, Clive Gillman, Board and
Curators would like to extend their deepest thanks
and appreciation to everyone who has helped
develop this exhibition and publication. First
and foremost, Camilla Løw for her wholehearted
commitment to the project. We are extremely
thankful to both Michael Archer and Dr Sarah
Lowndes whose texts contribute substantially to the
understanding of Camilla's practice and to Robert
Johnston for his sympathetic and elegant design of
this publication.

The exhibition would not have been possible
without the generous support and cooperation of:
Scottish Arts Council; Office for Contemporary Art,
Norway; The Royal Norwegian Consulate General,
Edinburgh; Pier Arts Centre, Orkney; Sutton Lane,
London/Paris & Elastic, Malmø; Maddalena and
Paolo Kind; Jens-Peter Brask; Nils Stærk and Ådne
Kverneland.

Camilla Løw would like to thank Will Bradley;
Elisabeth and Rune Løw; Krista and Norman Blake;
Kay and Simon Bolton.

Finally, we would like to thank everyone in the
DCA team who worked tirelessly to produce
Straight Letters.

DCA Dundee Contemporary Arts · Dundee City Council Changing for the Future · Scottish Arts Council · the Pier arts centre · NORWEGIAN CONSULATE GENERAL · OFFICE FOR CONTEMPORARY ART NORWAY

sing to me in french
michael archer

THE INTERACTION BETWEEN people and built or constructed form is central to Camilla Løw's work. 'Straight Letters', the title of this show, is an oblique reference to the distinctive style of graffiti that developed in São Paulo during the 1990s. Called *pixação*, its proponents (*pixações*) have adopted a kind of lettering based on Celtic runes. This has been done not through borrowing from the authentic source, but by appropriating a look from the cover artwork favoured by Goth metal bands. Quite unlike the florid, colourful imagery familiar from New York, São Paulo's buildings have become covered with an idiosyncratic black lettering that is at one and the same time contemporary, ancient, locally specific, international, direct, filtered, and above all culturally and personally expressive. A short online search brings up an image. It shows a boy spraying black paint onto the underside of a balcony. In order to reach up to this point he is standing on the shoulders of a boy, who is standing on the shoulders of a boy. The two lower boys are not gripping the person above them but are letting their arms hang loose at their sides. Everything looks effortless, natural. In another image a boy lies an unfeasibly long way over the edge of a tower block roof, bent at the waist so that he can reach as far down the façade of the building as possible with a long pole on the other end of which is a paint-loaded brush. Paint on concrete. Løw's work is in no way about this phenomenon, but its sensibility does connect with the gestural ambition, cultural acquisitiveness, and spatial authority of the *pixações*.

Løw puts paint on concrete, too. Perhaps this does not seem strange; after all, graffiti aside, we can see this sort of thing countless times every day on the façades of buildings and on workshop walls, ceilings and floors. The buildings look smarter, the workshops are less dusty, and people carry on the business of living safe in the knowledge that their surroundings are amenable and accommodating. But really, this putting of paint on concrete is remarkable and we should take some time to consider just why this is so.

The last essay Donald Judd wrote, published shortly after his death in 1994, was entitled 'Some aspects of colour in general, and red and black in particular'. He began it like this:

Material, space and colour are the main aspects of visual art. Everyone knows that there is material that can be picked up and sold, but no one sees space and colour. [1]

It is a statement full of Judd's characteristic bluntness that leaves no room for doubt: there are three aspects, everyone knows, no one sees. That he is both absolutely right about there being three aspects, and completely wrong about the fact that no one sees, is born out by Løw's sculpture. Material, space and colour are what she works with. If we attempt to keep to Judd's formula, Løw's material is concrete, oak, perspex and steel, the colour is the colour of the perspex and the paint with which she covers the oak and some of the concrete, and the space is the gallery within which she disposes the work. But we can't keep to the formula because it is really not possible to divide things up like that. The colours Løw uses are the basic ones — the primaries red, yellow and blue, together with black and white. They are Mondrian's colours, Rodchenko's colours, Newman's colours. Dan Flavin called red, yellow and blue Newman's 'simple problem', the problem as Newman saw it of rescuing those colours from the dogmatic 'idea-didact' they had become in the wake of their use by 'purists, neo-plasticists and other formalists'.[2] But for Mondrian, chief among the neo-plasticists, the primaries were not an idea at all. Quite the reverse. They were closest to reality and hence 'concrete'. In his last paintings, done in 1921 before he moved on to alternative ways of working, Rodchenko 'declared' pure red, yellow and blue as the three dimensions of colour. So in choosing to work with these colours Løw makes it amply clear that for her the three aspects of visual art are indivisible: colour is material is space. Actually, her blue is never primary blue. There's always an admixture of something else to make it a turquoise, as in *4 + 4*, a light blue, as in *High-rise*, or even a green, as in *Donna*. In general terms the colours she uses are potentially all colour and all tonality, as well as being illumination and shadow, light and dark. More specifically though, and especially given the greeniness of her blues, they do place her work very consciously in relation to Constructivist forms and ideas. When she speaks about her colour choice, Løw acknowledges this interest in Constructivism, though stresses that an important dimension to it is the degree to which women artists were major participants in the movement in the years leading up to and immediately following the Russian revolution. Rodchenko perhaps then, but more importantly Stepanova and Popova. And indeed Løw has titled works in honour of both these women in the past. In the *Productivist Manifesto* they co-wrote in 1921, Stepanova and Rodchenko insisted that both physical stuff and 'intellectual' materials such as light, colour, volume and space should all be treated

the same and understood as the material out of which art is produced.[3] Løw's sculpture emphasises the truth of this.

A feature of Løw's recent works is her use in them of one or more prefabricated, 30cm cube concrete blocks. Sufficiently large to assert a substantial presence, they are nonetheless small enough for her to be able to handle them with relative ease. Either on their own or in combination with an open, orthogonal framework made of painted, square-section oak they are suggestive of sculpture, monument, plinth, and architecture at one and the same time. A work such as *Unit* might seem to keep our attention within the gallery, its white frame atop a single block invoking both Brancusi's integral plinths and Sol LeWitt's *Variations of Incomplete Open Cubes*, but others leave us in no doubt that we need to draw on a much fuller sense of the urban experience if we are, in Judd's words, to 'see' how their material, colour and disposition both construct and articulate the space they inhabit. The way in which Løw deploys the blocks, stacking them in small columns of two, three, four or five, grouping works in the gallery rather than spacing them out evenly, invokes the tactile, immediate manner in which we find mutual accommodation between ourselves and the environment as we move through the city. The works' titles, too, allude to this. *Interchange, Exit, High-rise, Concrete, Arcade, Crossover*, all insistently place us in the street, or in those sites of domesticity, work and leisure that the street links together. And the street is a populated one: *Annalisa, Donna, Ramona, Tight Jeans* — there are bodies aplenty, and we don't need to know if they are personal friends, film characters, song lyrics, online avatars, product lines, advertising images or whatever, because any or all of these possibilities will be the right one.

Løw's sculpture is definite without being in the least rigid. It does not, for example, involve much in the way of fastening, joining or fixing. Suspension is sometimes necessary, as in the case of the linked perspex lozenges of *Ramona* or the three rectangular frames of *Digital*, not in order to immobilise them, but as a means to loosing form into space rather than having it all hug one or other surface of the gallery's containing volume. On the whole, things are placed, stacked, leant, and propped rather than bolted, screwed, glued or welded. *Annalisa, White Steel* and *Sister* do nothing more than rest against the wall, and the yellow shards of perspex that fringe the upper end of *Sister*'s long thin metal rod stay where they are merely due to friction. In doing so

they contrast strongly with the slump of wooden blocks threaded necklace-like onto the looped cord of *Diva*. The impression one has when amongst this work is that things are open to reconfiguration. It is not that *Diva*'s wooden blocks could be splayed in another arrangement, say, or that the bumps, dents and creases in the otherwise plain square metal sheet of *White Steel* could be either flattened out or alternatively developed into a more obviously functional shape. The work is too finely-judged for that. It is more that the energies flowing through the space brought into existence by Løw's installation of her work animate this endlessly mutable, plastic world. *Diva*'s slump, the jack-knife flip of *Arcade*'s diagonally-positioned black wooden frame, the delicate entanglement of the frames in *Broken Windows, Crossover*, and *Interchange*, the balance of *Donna*, the shifting patterns from face to face of *Stela* which pull the viewer round and round in search of that never-to-be-found definitive view — all of these speak to the reality of a world not of things but of forces and processes. There are meetings and divergences, moments of intensity juxtaposed with passages of calm and release, noise and aggression met with constructive silence. In part this mutability appears as a slipping between dimensionalities, not only line to plane to volume in actual space, but also into the virtual space of, say, the implied screens or pixels of *Digital*. Because for all that it is acutely aware of and sensitive to the histories of its forms and procedures, Løw's work unquestionably builds its arguments out of the fashions, predilections, and debates of the present moment.

1 Donald Judd, 'Some aspects of color in general and red and black in particular', *Artforum*, Summer, 1994, p. 70.

2 Barnett Newman quoted in Thomas B Hess, *Barnett Newman*, Tate Gallery, London, 1972, p. 77.

3 Varvara Stepanova & Alexander Rodchenko, *Productivist Manifesto*, 1921, reprinted in *Alexander Rodchenko*, Museum of Modern Art, Oxford, 1979, p. 130.

straight letters
Dr Sarah Lowndes

Yesterday, we went for a spin up the Haight — came across this homeless guy who wasn't begging — don't know how to explain it, but he had all his coppers and coins laid out on the ground in a perfect heart shaped peace sign.
Camilla Løw, email from San Francisco, 7th August 2005

PERHAPS THE MOST significant aspect of the work of Camilla Løw is the way in which she uses 'fixed' prefabricated materials such as wood and metal to articulate something about the heterogeneous quality of social life. Løw's work is articulated through an industrial and minimalist rubric, yet she moulds, joins and positions materials such as oak blocks, cast concrete, beaten brass, Plexiglas and mild-steel rod in forms that are recognisably human. Løw's work revisits the disciplined formalism of Russian Constructivism, De Stijl and Minimalism but the underlying impulse of her work lies in a consideration of the anthropometric qualities of sculpture. Her work can be seen as models of experienced action, witnessed on the street or at a bar or nightclub. Spelling out a heart shaped peace sign using coins is an act in some way similar to Løw's sculptural rearrangements of everyday materials into symbolic forms.

The titles of her works orient the viewer away from the industrial resonances of the materials, towards a consideration of the social implications of architecture and design. A low slanting fence of brightly painted wooden spurs jutting upwards from the gallery floor is entitled *Rum and Coke* (2003). An arrangement of two interconnected painted rectangular wooden frames balanced on a stack of three concrete blocks is named after the current retro fashion trend for *Tight Jeans* (2007). Often her sculptures have female names: *Viva*, *Donna*, *Annalisa*. Løw explains that these names are derived from various influences:

Sometimes it's a colour reference. Sometimes it's the shape or the attitude of the piece. I like to use names that suggest strong female characters. I think this has a lot to do with my sculptures often being minimal and maybe even masculine. It's also a direct link to the idea of the human scale in relation to architecture and the figure as the historical origin of sculpture.[1]

Løw's brand of Constructivism is not rigidly industrial, but closer to that of the playful rediscovery of those tropes by designers connected to the punk and post-punk scene in Manchester, such as Neville Brody and Peter Saville and Haçienda designer Ben Kelly. The interrelationship of performance and Constructivism found in Brody's and Saville's record sleeves and Kelly's bar and nightclub environments can be traced back to the roots of Russian Constructivism, and Varvara Stepanova and Liubov Popova's spindly geometric stage sets for Vsevolod Meyerhold's plays: respectively *The Death of Tarelkin* (1922) and *The Magnaminous Cuckold* (1922). These sets echoed the anatomy of the performers, demonstrating correspondences between human limbs and material as translated into model. The squares of Popova's framework, for example, are reinforced by X-shaped wooden batons, akin to arms that are crossed. The effect of the scaffold-like set rests not only on the particular material properties of the object (*faktura*) but also on the spatial presence of the object (*tektonika*): in other words, what material can become.

But although Løw's work evokes the human form, it does so in an abstract fashion — Daniel-Henry Kahnweiler's description of a Picasso sculpture of a free-floating arm could be applied here (Kahnweiler observed that the sculpture did not represent an arm but instead 'it represents armness').[2] Løw's work is not conventionally representational but instead articulates something of underlying reality. Løw's stylised 'figures' include *Donna* (2007), a slender painted wooden frame with a square, arm-like extension resting on two concrete blocks, and *Viva* (2004), which consists of lengths of wood threaded onto cord and hung up on the gallery wall like a collapsed marionette awaiting a puppeteer.[3] The stylization of Løw's figure surrogates generates a dialogue in her work between abstraction and representation. The attempt to depict figures as they were perceived was a major preoccupation of Alberto Giacometti, who considered that stylising the figure was the only way in which it was possible to 'grasp the ungraspable essence or core of human encounter'.[4] As John Paul Sartre noted in his famous essay on Giacometti, 'The Quest for the Absolute' (1948), this meant expressing a vision of the human as one who is seen by others: who exists in a social world.[5]

The life-like quality of Løw's sculptures is partially due to the way in which they are positioned. Rather than fix pieces with nails or glue, Løw installs her work as a balancing act.

Hanging, standing or leaning against the wall, the works investigate what might be seen as traditional sculptural or architectonic concerns with form, space, rhythm, tension, balance and the properties of materials.[6]

These properties are demonstrated by a series of works including *Seven* (2004) and *Sister* (2006) made by threading coloured Plexiglas onto mild-steel rod to create jagged multi-coloured 'heads' on a spare and elongated stem. These top-heavy stylised figures are propped against gallery walls as witnesses to the action that unfolds within the exhibition space. Suspended works such as *Viva* (2004), *Soledada Red* (2004) and *Diva* (2006) dangle from a single nail. Other works result from various components that are linked and balanced, such as *Crossover* (2007), which consists of two interconnected painted wooden frames, one of which rests on a single concrete cube.

This piece brings back the idea of making the piece less autonomous — I mean, it has the function of being able to be placed either way on the concrete cube. I guess this is a way of trying to make the piece more mobile, yet it's definitely 'unmovable'. The piece is only placed on top of the cube, and not fastened to it — like all my work.[7]

Løw imbues her installations with a palpable kinetic edge, as the viewer must not only look at the work but also navigate around the pieces, physically discovering the space with their body.[8] In this too, Løw's work returns to the performative aspect of De Stijl reference points — such as El Lissitzky's *Proun Room* (1923) which was intended to jolt the viewer out of their sense of separation from the work. Lissitzky commented that 'if on previous occasions in his march-past in front of the picture-walls, he was lulled by the painting into a certain passivity, now our design should make the man active. This should be the purpose of the room.'[9]

Recently, Løw has begun working with cast concrete, to produce cube forms, which are then arranged in the space in humanlike columns, such as *Stela* (2007), an industrial totem pole composed from five stacked concrete cubes. Again a 'corrupted' Minimalism is applied, to allow the corporeal aspect of an industrial material to speak. Discussing these works Løw explains,

The concrete cubes are 30 × 30 × 30cm — a size that relates to the industrial use of concrete, but at the same time, designed and made specifically for an art purpose. I started including the concrete cubes quite recently. I think I was looking for a new material where it made sense to repeat the form over and over again. I was looking for a way of making modules that could be placed in direct relation to the space itself. The wooden pieces I make in my studio are more autonomous in the way that they are

difficult to alter after they've been made. They are also labour intensive. By using the concrete, I felt I could be more playful on-site.[10]

These recent works made using concrete cubes are 'figure surrogates' in the manner of Robert Morris's *Two Columns* (1961).[11] Morris's mandate for the development of sculpture 'Notes on Sculpture: Part I and II' (1966)[12] and Michael Fried's famous counter-attack 'Art & Objecthood' (1967), are so well-known they hardly need to be discussed in detail here, except to make the point that the qualities that Fried identified as so problematic in the work of Morris and Donald Judd (site-specificity, temporality, 'theatricality') are precisely those that have shaped what might be called the performative sculpture of Løw and other artists who have emerged since the late 80s from the Sculpture & Environmental Art department at Glasgow School of Art including Claire Barclay, Martin Boyce and Jim Lambie. The Department, until recently run by David Harding, adopted the unofficial motto 'Context is half the work' drawn from John Latham and Barbara Stevini's 1965 Artists' Placement Group and supported the growth of site-specific and installation work, encouraging students to make work 'with and through people'.

The way in which the meanings of cultural reference points shift through time and use is a constant theme in Camilla Løw's work, which makes her choice of title for this exhibition particularly resonant. 'Straight Letters' is a reference to the distinctive etiolated *pixação* letterforms, which cover the exteriors of many of the buildings in São Paulo. As François Chastanet has described

The São Paolo milieu is unique because, unlike most other American, European and even Asian graffiti scenes, which reproduce New York letterforms more or less faithfully, the pixacões have developed a totally different imaginary calligraphy.[13]

The *pixação* script contains elements of Nordic and Celtic runes and Germanic black letter type as these were the inspiration for the graphics of 1970s and 80s Heavy Metal bands such as Iron Maiden and Slayer. These, rather than Hip-hop, were the music of the street culture in São Paulo in the 1980s. There is an obvious correlation between the spare lines of Camilla's Løw's 'figure surrogates' and these segmented, rune-like vertical letters.

In the last year Løw has returned to live in her home city of Oslo, after periods spent living and working in Glasgow, and then San Francisco. It seems no coincidence that after returning to Scandinavia, she has developed a body of work partially inspired by ancient runic inscriptions.[14] A peculiarity of the runic alphabet as compared to the Old Italic family is the relative absence of horizontal strokes — the angular shape of the 24 runic letters was designed for ease of carving against the grain of narrow pieces of wood (the 'scrap paper' of forested Europe).[15] The rune-like *pixação* letters share this vertical characteristic, as curves and horizontal lines are also difficult to render with a paint roller while balancing on a window ledge of a tower block. The thinness and verticality of *pixação* letterforms also gives them a formal resemblance to the stick-like figures of Giacometti. David Sylvester observed of Giacometti's sculptures: 'They are figures without physical superfluousness [...] their thinness a 'condensation'.[16] Runes and *pixação* similarly represent a condensation of meaning into figure, an expression of significant form.[17] The carved wood and the quickly applied paint are made to speak something of the underlying reality of existence. The significant form they evoke reappears constantly in Camilla Løw's work: not the human figure, but the shadow that it casts.

1   Camilla Løw, in response to questions sent by the author, December 17th 2007.

2   Daniel-Henry Kahnweiler, *The Sculptures of Picasso* (London: 1949), quoted in Andrew Causey, *Sculpture Since 1945* (Oxford and New York: Oxford University Press, 1998), p. 34.

3   This interpretation of the work appears in Dan Fox, 'Camilla Low', *Frieze Yearbook 2005/6* (London: Frieze Publications, 2005).

4   Christian Klemm, Notes to accompany the exhibition 'Alberto Giacometti' (New York: Museum of Modern Art, 2001), p. 7.

5   John Paul Sartre, 'The Quest for the Absolute' (1948), in English translation *Essays in Esthetics*, Wade Baskin, ed., (London: 1964), p. 101.

6   Camilla Løw, in response to questions sent by the author, November 8th 2007.

7   Camilla Løw, in response to questions sent by the author, December 17th 2007.

8   The phrase 'discovering the space with their body' is a paraphrase of a statement by the American artist George Trakas, made in relationship to his seminal works *The Piece That Went Through the Floor* (1970) and *The Piece That Went Through the Window* (1970), both of which were installed at 112 Greene Street in New York. Trakas said, 'In my work I wanted to confront the spectators directly and draw them in physically to discover space with their bodies.' George Trakas

interviewed by Hugh M. Davis and Sally E. Yard in Davies and Yard, *George Trakas Log Mass: Mass Culture* (Amhearst: University Gallery, University of Masachusetts, 1980) quoted in Julie H. Reiss, *From Margin to Center: The Spaces of Installation Art* (Cambridge, Massachusetts: The MIT Press, 1999), p. 120.

9   El Lissitzky quoted in Nancy J. Troy, *The De Stijl Environment* (Cambridge, Massachusetts: The MIT Press, 1983), p. 126, quoted in Julie H. Reiss, *From Margin to Center: The Spaces of Installation*, op. cit., p. 120.

10   Camilla Løw, in response to questions sent by the author, December 17th 2007.

11   'In the perception of relative size, the human body enters into the total continuum of sizes and establishes itself as a constant on that scale. One knows immediately what is smaller and larger than the self and the two are seen differently because of the different qualities of intimacy in relation to its size'. Robert Morris, 'Notes on Sculpture: Part II', *Artforum*, October 1966.

12   'The better new work takes the relationships out of the work and makes them a function of space, light and the viewer's field of vision. The object is but one of the terms in the newer aesthetic. It is in some ways more reflexive because one's awareness of oneself existing in the same space as the work is stronger than in previous work, with its many internal relationships.' Robert Morris, 'Notes on Sculpture: Part II', Ibid.

13   François Chastanet, 'The Architecture of São Paulo, Brazil is covered by a unique form of calligraphic grafitti' (2001) http://eyemagazine.com/feature.php?id=123&fid=540 accessed November 8th, 2007.

14   'About 5,000 [runic] inscriptions survive, mainly memorial stone carvings and owner declarations scratched onto metal objects, dating from about AD 100 to 1600. The majority come from Sweden: 1,000 from Norway; about 700 from Denmark; and the rest mainly from Germany, the British Isles, and Ireland.' David Sacks, *The Alphabet* (London: Hutchinson, 2003), p. 150.

15   David Sacks, *The Alphabet*, Ibid., p. 149.

16   David Sylvester, 'Perpetuating the Transient' (London: Arts Council Gallery, 1955), reprinted in David Sylvester, *About Modern Art* (London: Chatto & Windus, 1996), pp. 52–53.

17   'Significant form' is a term that first appeared in Clive Bell, *Art* (London: Chatto & Windus, 1914).

CamILLa LØW
Born 1976, Norway

1998–2001 Glasgow School of Art
· 1996–1998 Asker Kunstskole

SOLO EXHIBITIONS
2008 'Straight Letters', Dundee Contemporary Arts*
'Straight Letters' Pier Arts Centre, Orkney*
2007 'Broken Windows', Elastic Gallery, Malmø
2006 'Henriette Grahnert/Camilla Løw', Sutton Lane, Paris
2005 'Camilla Løw', Jack Hanley Gallery, San Francisco
2004 'Camilla Løw', Sutton Lane, London

SELECTED group EXHIBITIONS
2007 'Language of Vision', Middlesbrough Institute of Modern Art, Middlesbrough*
StatoilHydro — Art Grant, Kunstnerforbundet, Oslo*
'The Corny Show — AKA The Art is in the Heart', Karma International, Zurich*
'Dump: Postmodern Sculpture in the Dissolved Field', The National Museum of Art,
Architecture and Design, Oslo*
'How To Improve the World — Sixty Years of British Art', Gas Hall, Birmingham
'Robert Smithson', Vårutstillingen 2007, Fotogalleriet, Oslo
2006 'How to Improve the World — Sixty Years of British Art', Hayward Gallery, London*
'Try Again. Fail Again. Fail Better.', Momentum, 4th Nordic Festival of Contemporary Art,
Galleri F15, Moss, Norway*
'Endless Summer', Westlondonprojects, London
'60 — Sixty Years of Sculpture in the Arts Council Collection', Longside Gallery, Yorkshire
Sculpture Park
2005 'Blankness Is Not a Void', Standard (Oslo), Oslo, Norway
'Shadows and Prisms', The Print Studio, Glasgow
'Sutton Lane in Paris', c/o Galerie Ghislaine Hussenot, Paris
'Contemporary Nordic Sculpture 1980–2005', Wanås Foundation, Sweden*
2004 'Invaggio', Museo Corta Alta, Fossembrone, Italy
'Britannia Works', The British Council, Athens*
'Synth', Kunstraum B/2, Leipzig, Germany*
'Solar Lunar', Doggerfisher, Edinburgh
2003 'The Echo Show', Tramway, Glasgow*
'East International', Norwich Gallery*
'Greyscale/CMYK', Royal Hibernian Academy, Dublin*
2002 'The Shadows', Transmission Gallery, Glasgow
'Greyscale/CMYK', Tramway, Glasgow*
Switch Space Gallery, Glasgow (Two-person show with Ursula Nistrup)

* indicates publication

Gallery 1

Nova, 2008
Concrete & paint, 120 × 30 × 30cm

Broken Windows, 2007
Wood, paint & cord, 50 × 50 × 50cm
Elastic Collection, Malmö

Donna, 2007
Wood, paint & concrete, 180 × 85 × 30cm
Kverneland Collection, Stavanger

Stela, 2008
Concrete & paint, 150 × 30 × 30cm

Crossover, 2007
Wood, paint & concrete, 137 × 127 × 75cm
Brask Collection, Copenhagen

Tight Jeans, 2007
Wood, paint & concrete, 189 × 30 × 30cm
Nils Stærk, Copenhagen

Gallery 2

White Steel, 2008
Metal & spray paint, 125 × 125cm

Sister, 2006
Perspex & metal rod, 260 × 60 × 50cm

Interchange, 2008
Wood, paint & concrete, 132 × 66 × 60cm

Concrete, 2008
Wood, paint & concrete, 180 × 30 × 30cm

High-rise, 2008
Wood, paint & concrete, 240 × 30 × 30cm
The National Museum of Art, Architecture and
Design, Oslo

Exit, 2008
Wood, paint & concrete, 180 × 30 × 30cm
The National Museum of Art, Architecture and
Design, Oslo

Arcade, 2008
Wood, paint & concrete, 150 × 53 × 46cm
StatoilHydro Art Collection, Norway

Unit, 2008
Wood, paint & concrete, 120 × 30 × 30cm

Diva, 2006
Wood & cord, 200 × 115 × 63cm

Ramona, 2008
Perspex & metal, 520 × 80 × 80cm

4 + 4, 2005
Wood & paint, 139 × 9 × 9cm
The Pier Arts Centre Collection, Orkney acquired
through the National Collecting Scheme for
Scotland with assistance from the National Fund for
Acquisitions.

Digital, 2008
Wood, paint & cord, 270 × 90 × 90cm

Ancillary Space

Untitled (Black), 2008
Screenprint, edition 30, 100 × 70cm
(Yellow edition not exhibited)

Annalisa, 2006
Wood & paint, 210 × 5.4 × 5.4cm

Also illustrated:

Viva, 2004
Wood & cord, 220 × 40 × 30cm
Kind Family Trust, London

Installation view, Gallery 2

Gallery 2: **White Steel & Digital**

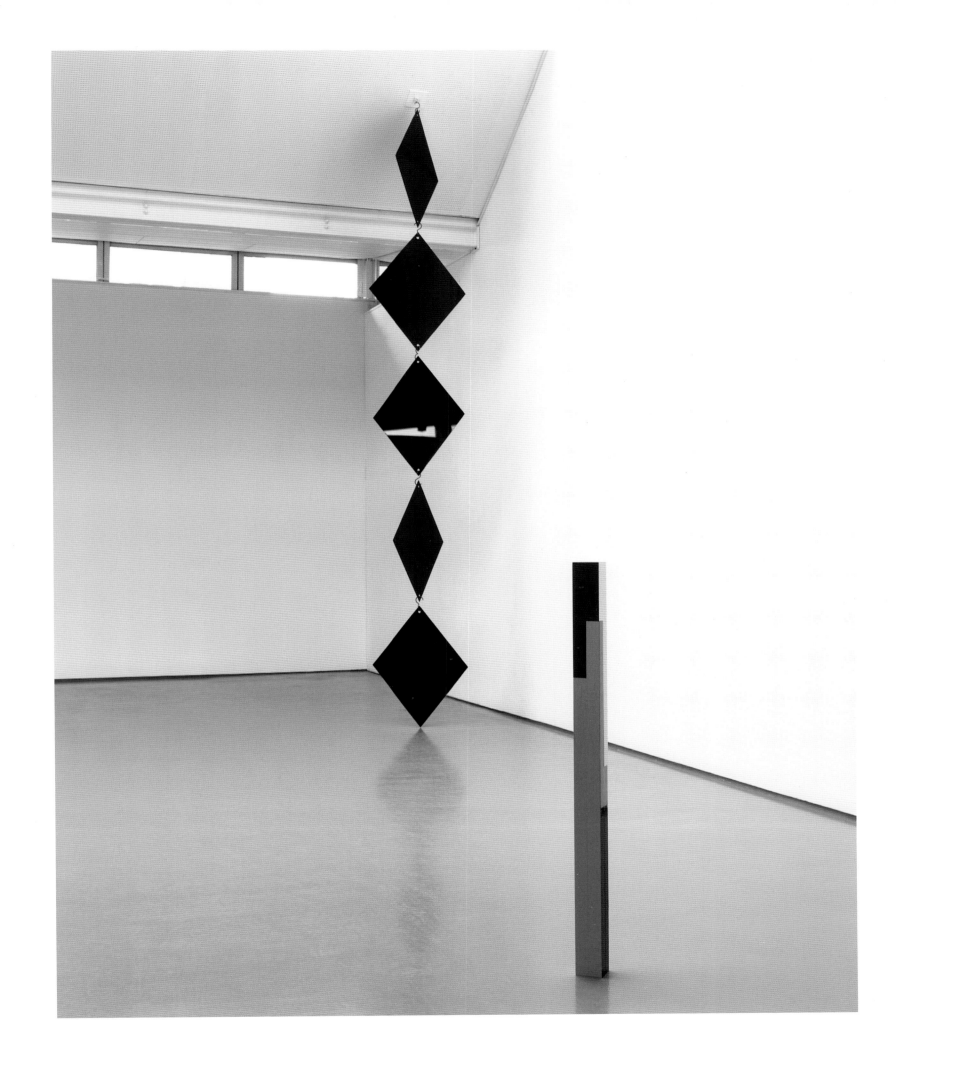

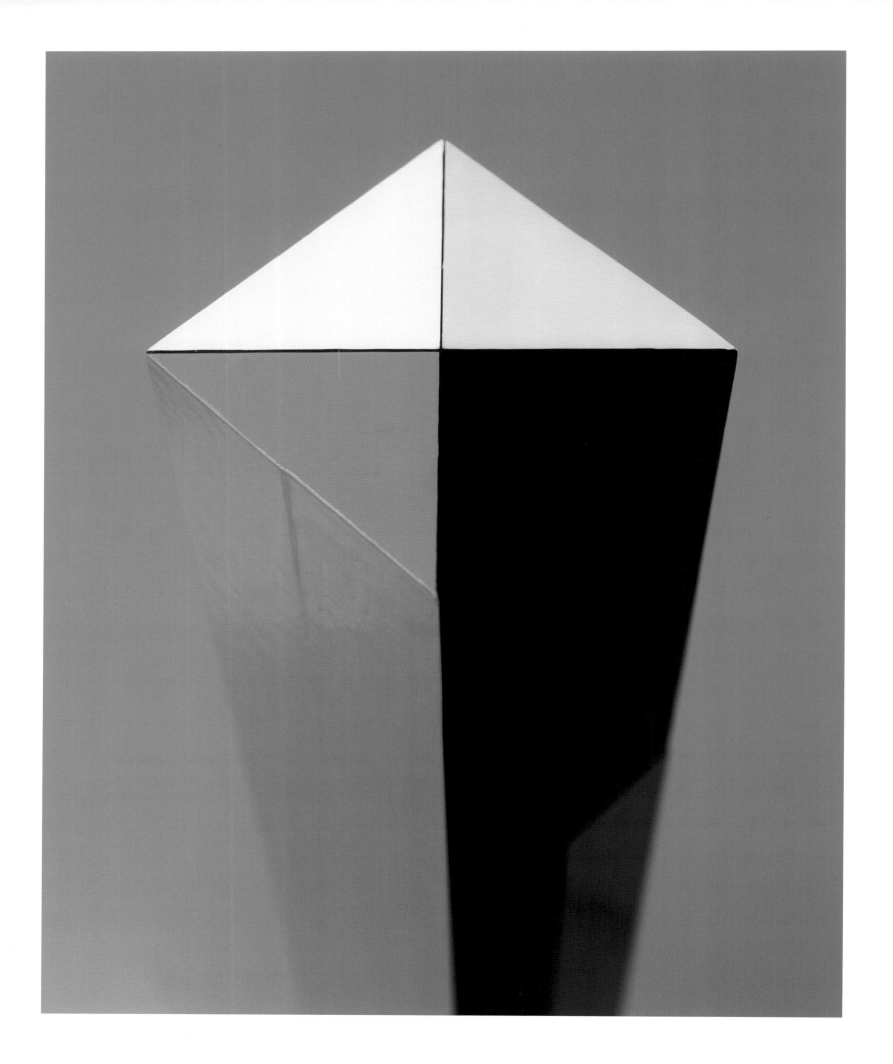

4 + 4 (detail)

Installation view, Gallery 2

Over: Installation view, Gallery 1

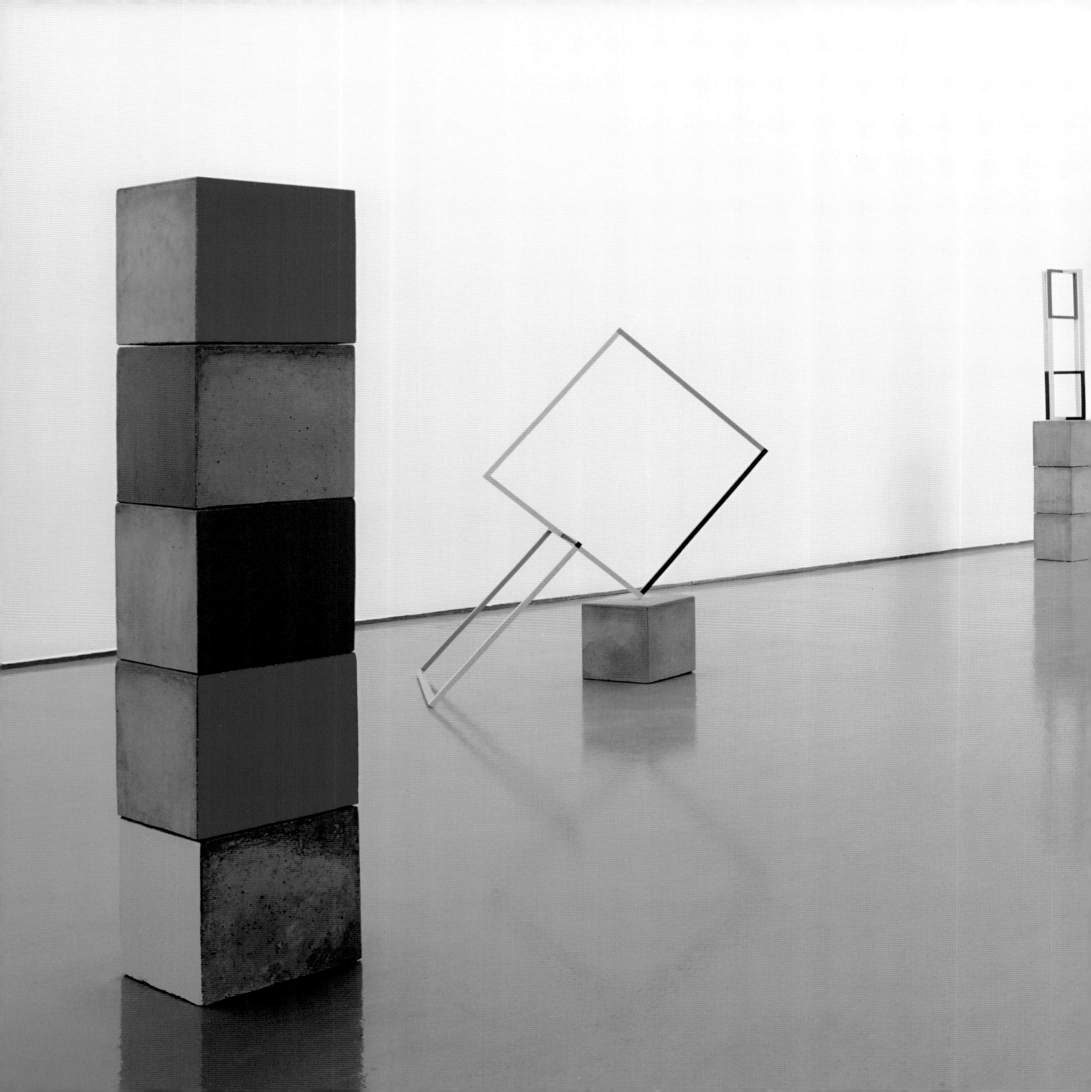

Gallery 1: **Stela & Crossover**

Tight Jeans

Over: Nova

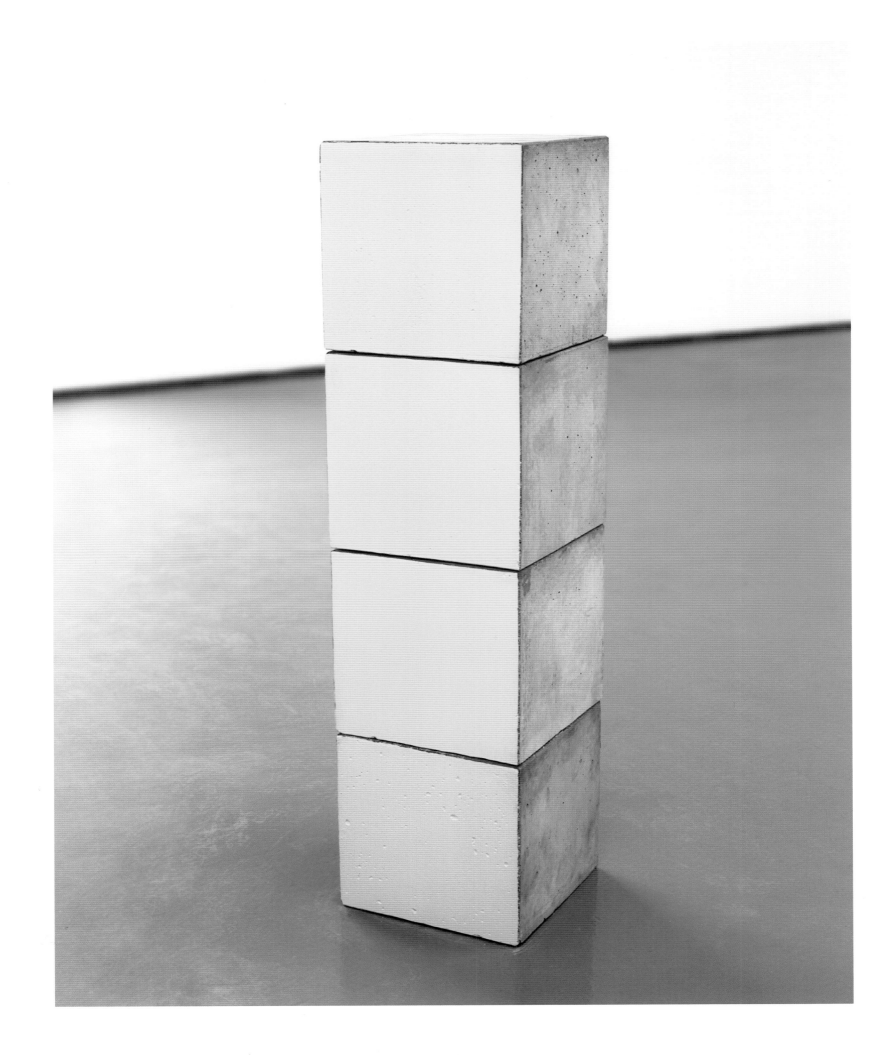

Ancillary Space: **Annalisa & Untitled (Black)**   Over: **Viva & Diva**

White Steel

Over: Unit & Interchange

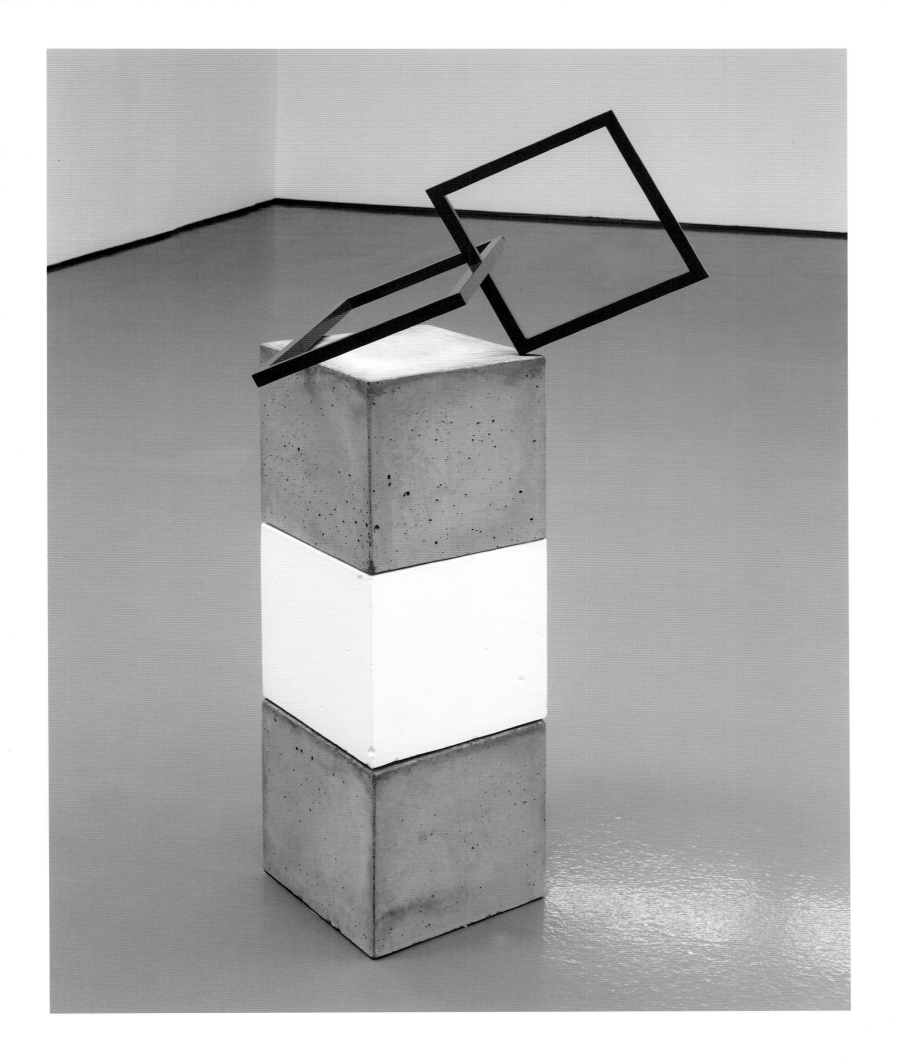

Gallery 2: **Ramona, High-rise, 4 + 4, Digital**

Installation view, Gallery 2

Installation view, Gallery 2

Gallery 2: Sister & Interchange